Covalence

COVALENCE

by

Joseph Zealberg

THE HILARY THAM CAPITAL COLLECTION
Selections for 2015 by Michael Klein

THE WORD WORKS
WASHINGTON, D.C.

Acknowledgments

Grateful acknowledgment is made to *qarrtsiluni* for publication of "In the Middle of the Bench," where the poem first appeared in slightly different form, and to *The Sow's Ear Poetry Review*, for publishing "The Lesson."

My deepest gratitude goes to my entire family, my friends, my professional colleagues and associates, my teachers, and all the patients and veterans with whom I have had the privilege to work.

In addition, my heartfelt thanks go to Richard Garcia, poet, teacher, and mentor; to the Long Table Poets of Charleston; and to The Poetry Society of South Carolina.

I am exceptionally grateful to Michael Klein for choosing this book for the Hilary Tham Capital Collection.

Finally, my greatest thanks go to Nancy White, for her editorial guidance, wisdom, and patience.

Contents

SYNTHESIS

COVALENCE

Sometimes you wake up and the night moans like an animal in pain.
I sent a text message to Walt Whitman, asking for help in
        translating this sound.
We were neighbors after all, watching each other across the
        Delaware.
I couldn't find him beneath my work boots, or inside the avenue's
        concrete sidewalks.
But his atoms advised that life is the covalence of lunacy and love.

Let me not write the asterisk of a stanza's ordinary pain.
This is memory's alembic, its whispered encasement: Thereof.
As I embrace the bonds of suffering and praise,
memorize the membranes of a father's and mother's people,
I speak the analogue language of a mint leaf's tongue.

I collect discounted dolls, moldy beds, wrinkled shoes lost.
Here, the human sclera dims and dulls to a question-brow.
And on this route an end-barge is tossed into shadows and drowns.
Let me scroll along fields of kingdoms come and kingdoms departed,
where a peach blossom shivers—aware of the coming frost.

ORIGINS

A FEW PARTS OF SELF

My helices derive from nightmares where men of the house
spoke ghosts through ears, from T-shirts ripped
and spotted red, sirens at night as I stood in the crib
and shook the wooden rails, shook them from dreams,
ruining plans. I was afraid Zorro and Ramar of the Jungle
might take me green into clouds of Stetson hats, bottles
of Ortlieb's beer, donated nouns, purple eyes, silver El trains.
I arise from haunted Carpathian hills and camps of sin
where heads deloused in kerosene, where castles
threw stones, where gypsy tents invited you down
to take a chair, to taste the knowledge: how you will end.
I proceed from diesel fumes and shoeshine kits, union strikes,
gang fights after school on playground turf, swinging belts,
buckles, fists, sawed-off bats and bricks. I emanate
from step-ball games and splats of pigeon shit, factory smoke
on window sills, coughs of coagulated blood, seamstress pins,
denture folks who gnawed depression lard and mustard
shot on bread, from old clothes turned to new, hot dog
meals on Christmas Day with Spam mixed in, laughter at
fever's praise, the tall drifts of urban tarnished snow.

PIATRA NEAMŢ, 1931

The Romanian girl recovers from intestinal worms. They've eased from her body to rest on the ground. Her wavy black hair fears such tendrils. She dreams gefilte fish, honey and lemon. She sews her dolls from cloth remnants. A deaf-mute poet arrives in the park. Russet hair tops his Carpathian gyrations. Tangential to nothing, he visits each bench and writes a poem for every adult person. His ¾ length coat, warm and woolen, recalls aromas of apple cake spices. Once, the girl heard a rabbi say: Petre, the deaf-mute poet, can teach a squirrel to speak like Moses. At an old table, a *ţigan* finishes eating her eggplant salad. She places bent cards face-up on the table, then performs divination upon unleavened bread. The pattern reveals that shadows will lacerate the sun. Ice tongs will dress in brown-pressed buttons. Potatoes will lose their uneven eyelids. People will survive on marrow and tapioca. The deaf-mute poet will ride a bookmark's lining. He'll sleep until stones become pictures and games. Until a guillotined moon becomes whole again, the Romanian girl will sew earth-string pellets of shame.

ZALMAN AND SIMA, ROMANIA, 1938

Soon they'll be fixed inside the sun's pox.
Gypsy music turned eclipse, violins to fire.
Dark complexions mutate into chitin, chalk.
They're so relaxed, thinking in dreams. Posed
for this portrait, side by side, brother, sister.
Greek statue faces, hair as dark as blindness.
Their hearts will travel grated ways of apples
knocked from branches, crushed and cracked
above dry dirt, broken beneath a glass swing.
Their arched brows maintain summits of hope.
Lips, mouths, eyes: Biblical-full. How will
siblings hide their nausea, postpone the silence
needed in the gleam of Jewish exoskeletons?
How will they betray the straits of absent shoes
approaching songs, hidden lungs, and skin,
if their soles are barely wrinkled, barely worn?

NOVEMBER 12, 1950

Sunday in Kentucky: Fort Knox. Scopolamine
made my mother rinse the baby in her dreams.

The baby had died, she believed, hidden,
while a nurse watched a cherry bomb explode.

Across the infant's inner heel, a play was written
in a patter of *La mulți ani*. The star was penned

by a careless army surgeon. He believed
that the child would exsanguinate one day

in the time it took to mix a spoonful of Ovaltine
into a glass of cold milk. In the Syracuse Herald-American,

Sergei Uritsky announced that the Russians had dropped
an atomic bomb over Syracuse, New York.

A photo of the cloud resembled a giant version
of Walt Whitman's hat, suspended over a skyscraper-sized can.

The poorly designed mushroom smoke was riding
like a puff of cream over broken buildings,

burned to recognizable strictures and dirt.
This destruction was a bad day in the south and north,

an evil rise for tanks and dogs. Meanwhile
the surgeon blessed the baby's eyes with silver nitrate.

This prevented blindness, Biblical boils.
Apgar scores weren't conceived for two more years.

In a tin-can trailer, my sergeant father went to sleep.
He woke up after ancient deeds. Gold remained

behind bunkers and wires, surveillance cameras. Ingots swelled
until James Bond arrived with Oddjob and Pussy Galore.

Goldfinger couldn't comprehend the Geiger counter's reason
as I rode toward Camden on Walt's dusty hat.

SHORT BUT SWEET

On the morning of my circumcision
the Mohel required a magnifying glass.
Perhaps it was cold that day, frigid, sub-zero.
My parents explained, Yes, it was November, in the hills.
They remember a stag behind a hemlock, heavy with ice.
Was this an omen or a dreamed excuse?
I thought my therapist had cured this obsession.
Yet I often dream that my wife complains, says she wants sex
in the back of the car, but still expects me to drive.
Then I feel the desire to defend myself. I want to say,
in Junior High they called me King Kong, Meat Bat,
Elephant Guy in Heat. I want to brag. I want to cry.
I tell her, We can make seated love, rodeo style
in the open trunk, on top of the spare tire
and I'll still be able to reach the steering wheel.
This could be bad sleep apnea or penile fiction.
In the recurring dream, she calls me Small Boy.
Runt Hose. Pencil Point Stud. Then she walks out,
smelling good. I hear the click of her red high heels
and my blood pressure seems to rise. When I wake,
I sweat and scratch at my arms. What can a guy do?
I grab a beer, then listen to Elton John's "Rocket Man,"
Tom Waits' plaintive tune "Hold On," or
"Waiting for the Miracle" by Leonard Cohen.

ALMOST FIVE

Down Mrs. Snag's front porch, he saw brigades
of maggots crowd a dead bird's eye. How queer
to see the little globe missing, gone, a weird
bone orbit to its inner tunnel there.

He'd never looked at death before, but soon
it churned the sparrow's belly dancing 'round.
He squatted near those drying feathers, torn,
no movement of its beak. No wings or sound.

Was this the source that kept him full of fright—
so hazed he could not sleep, those demons crawl-
ing into dawn, all daytime fearing night?

From crown to claw alone, forms stiff and fell,
earth's course will say to everything goodbye.
He recognized time's gray monopoly.

ONE DONE, ONE NEARLY GONE

Let me tell you what my tombstone read:

A jug of wine, a thimbleful of air, now you, my love . . .

I thought about the ace of spades, its silicon taste,

the view from a creek's bottom, its hungry fish sounds.

Mother tasted my demise from a tower of thorns.

Father wondered, What are we doing, interviewing the dead?

I was watching how a flower cries. If dandelions sweat,

how do stones reassure each visitor's hand in the lockdown smile

of a passing bird? I bloomed in red from forehead lines.

Nothing bad or good, just foreign ground, cinnamon hands.

Trees filled with hearts. Letters piercing wet cement tongues.

DOUBLE PNEUMONIA, 1954

A headless boy parachutes down
through a black and white silent film.
Pine needles, inserted through his ears.
Doctors say there's insurrection in his blood.

His disembodied head is the main chute's
convex fluff. Face is stretched
like a rubber sheet, his eyes squint
from the top of a luminous shroud.
There is no pain, just unexpected dizziness.

He can't see lattice ground or lettuce farms
spiraling below. A turkey vulture passes by.
So red, its glider face. The bird of prey advises,
Do not roll if you touch the earth too hard.

Silk suspension lines
are made of run-on sentences,
verbs of arteries and veins.
What would Popeye do without his spinach can?

Spartan, wise, he shouldn't complain.
Cirrus clouds, clearly frost and visible,
boil a needle and syringe in curdled milk.

He thinks a bomb or maybe flak had hit the fuselage.
Where's the open neck, his rubber oxygen mask?
The fog of VapoRub is closing down his thorax.

Will it matter to the birds if he yells Geronimo
to find the mouth and lungs orbiting the sun?
Maybe that's the doctors' lousy plan.
Combat boots will act as guides for penicillin.

WAR STORIES

When she cooks memory and scrambled eggs,
Mother's genesis from Piatra Neamț
stands until life in Philadelphia glimmers
with matzo and apples. Sour cream cakes

run glaze down Carpathian mountain wings
with wine flowing, aged *brinza*. She, a chosen
chaperoned queen of the ball, danced wavy hair
every night until brown potato shirts screamed

like bulging bags of heavy-booted hornets.
They twice-killed the rabbi's little sons
poised upon his knees so he could watch
the sky, those shirts let him go like a soup bone,

allowed his Psalter beard to live in apostasy.
His Torah flew like a buzzard. A Greek friend
gave birth after two days of labor, her husband's
cloud-eyes went for baby's breath in a field or not

where brown shirts spiraled in mud heat, stung
his Jewish marrow into *mamaliga* mush piles,
pushed his man-something into cold remains
of palate, raised his stiff shame in silent ruins.

Bouquets of honey flame and dead flags
soaked chamomile perfume, eyelids sewn.
Those shirts spilled cream of Mother's heart.
They issued buzzing, human claim, sizzled hope.

TRIANGLE

He seldom comes straight home.
She's widowed by the Old Spot's tap.

Fatigue caps, long-sleeve flannel shirts
hang from hooks behind the closet door.

One plays fire trucks and flashlight leads.
Summer brings their week-long joke.

Listen for the steel-toed shoes,
squeaks of leather over third-floor steps.

Rearrange the ashtray by a quarter inch.
Cook that favorite meal: sauerkraut,

mashed potatoes, Oscar Mayer hot dogs.
Civil shine surrounds his razor-polished army face.

He often eats alone. Then he salts his beer.
Shadow war of drink, a whiskey glass.

One sip inaugurates blood.
At night, the screaming sex of ambulance.

ONLY CHILD

1.

I told my brother who did not exist
I want my last year back.
This was my terrible secret.
Being the doorknob that he was,
he couldn't keep anything confidential.

My fictional sister,
the hanging art glass chandelier,
locked me into wall-to-wall darkness,

and my identical twin,
the yellow giraffe made of velvet and glue,
taught me to look at the sun for God.

The rosebush, my cousin,
thriving in our fenced backyard,
produced buds and hope in folded red,
lessons on dancing with thorns.

2.

This: my rosebush, a folded darkness.
The sun taught lessons of yellow secrets.
Being with the sun, identical,
I wanted wall-to-wall rosebushes,
chandeliers and thorns.

The velvet glass told me
that the knob and fenced-in backyard
keep the fictional toward the confidential.

Now I exist inside a chandelier.
Not confidential, I twist inside a yellow god.

And brother, our door, toward that year,
made me keep secrets and lessons.
But not anything of you, my sister,
my terrible dancing twin.

TURNING THE DREAM

Again, a clap of bells, the cloud of red smoke.
Behind the purple steel octopus, we meet.
This is where peace ends.
You have my father's hands;
explain what you've done to his hair.

You float like some invertebrate,
shoulders down in a glass tank's turbulent green.
I try to pay you off with a twenty-dollar bill.
You bleed charcoal dust and oil my sleeve.
What do you hear from that flat wooden spoon?

Your black fingernail toys with the artery's pulse
inside my neck. The beat says: No way out.
I chant: Baklava, Hullabaloo, Brouhaha.
I need Moses or Christ, but only items
from a shopping list emerge in prayer.

Pickled herring. Canned sardines. Buttermilk and jam.
Are you a fish or shark? Man or dream?
Do you care if that spider rappels from your tongue?
You demand a jigger of Seagram's, suck the burn
from a straw made of paper-wasp walls.

Baklava, Hullabaloo, Brouhaha.
How can you chew that wind-up plastic beetle?
Offended now, you ask if I have a legal will.
I bequeath an old black pen, a Slinky toy,
a vase for my children. But I'm a boy; I have no children.

Eyelashes or snakes? Eyelashes or snakes?
At the chemistry lab, I mix ginkgo with vinegar skin,
wax and sulfur. Instead of legs: you wobble around
on stacked blue cups. Instead of boots, you immerse
those tagged toes in Mason jars of glue.

I rap a poem about The Old Woman Who Lived in a Shoe
and you slap down another shot. I splash sludge
below your scars with cologne and Listerine.
Time for dinner! you command. You desire
anchovy pizza, Greek salad, a keg of beer.

You'll spare me if I make the call.
Turning the dream,
I am recognized, recognized, recognized—
Baklava, Hullabaloo, Brouhaha.
I must also kiss your mole.

SHADOW BOXERS

Sometimes the ratchet worked our neck bones.
Fracture lines, sweetness spilled.
God had clubbed us down with taproom curses,
filled the room on Friday nights.
Reds and blues unshelved themselves.
Weeping sticks. Slapping rain.
The Lord became irregularity.
We spoke as purple statues, volutes of patina mold.
God was dark and pupillary.
Mirrors prayed *cum sanctus spiritus*, crossed themselves.
Branches timed the Lord's unsettled name.
Below three floors of bricks,
the moon inhaled each nettled word.
God had placed His bets on neither one of us.
And for this crime that wasn't criminal,
He winked behind the moon.
Now we fit, move along.
We dream of the second hand.

EARLY CONVERSATION ON THE SOUL'S SURTAX

Father says, You're dead the moment you are born.
I hunt through army discharge papers,
ask his mother's favorite flower during World War II.

His oldest brother's name was James
and not Augustus. Now I'm almost there.
Mother offers legal folders, yellow wills.

Inspection and approval. Windows evaporate.
Instructions signed by a notary's
death-pressed seal.

This fact enters a million generations.
Cathedral clouds and synagogues blow the shofar.
I dance in the middle of a crucifix sentence,

drink its polished empty desk and chair.
On a cardboard box, "Revelations" is written
in red. I'm batting in a cage of alias phantoms.

Maturity begins when you don't ask safe questions.
And if you understand the freezing point of tears,
one thousand museums will be needed.

WHAT WAS THAT ORANGUTAN'S NAME?

Remember what it was like living below
the Benjamin Franklin Bridge? We played
ball tag with rope and El trains' wheels, inhaled
blue-gray dreams from PTC bus tailpipes.
And that crackpot at Wimpy's White Tower near K&A,
he'd fix Cherry Cokes, put boogies on our straws.
Mrs. Fischer made good homemade lemonade
and kept a surgical mask on her Dracula doll.
On July 4th, 1965, that musky mutant orangutan
with a vast Napoleonic complex made an escape
from the Philadelphia Zoo. Remember how
he took the trolley down Girard Avenue, hailed
a shiny Yellow Cab, then boarded
Admiral Dewey's flagship, docked a block away
from the rusty span along the shipping piers?
Remember that hairy beast-man? He wanted
to study acting, to become a movie star, to rekindle
the Spanish-American War. That wiry dumb-dumb
ordered the main cannons of the USS Olympia
to fire across the Delaware. Then we hitchhiked
along I-95 heading north toward Bristol, where other
escaped primates were stomping Pall Mall cigarettes
and drinking buttered rum and kegs of Schmidt's Beer.
I think a cop named Frank drove us back to City Hall
where we took the slow narrow elevator to the top
of the giant statue of William Penn. The tall
wire fence kept us secure, 500 feet above Market Street
and Broad. Flocks of pigeons escaped from clouds
and mansard windows. Journalists from the *Inquirer*,
fearful of psycho monkey troupes, rolled up
those canvas tops of their '57 Chevy Bel Airs.
The city's anaerobic sewer gas smelled
like licorice and Three Musketeers candy bars.

I wanted devil's food cupcakes from Horn & Hardart's
but Mom invited that orange-haired admiral for dinner.
Remember how strange and cold it was that night?
Mom made that monkey-man a peace-offering: eggs
over easy, Habbersett's scrapple, French-fried plantains.
Remember how she drove the orangutan to the airport?
He looked hairy and strange stumbling up the stairs
before he embarked to St. Helena's Island. I wonder
how he arranged his escape to Hollywood, California?
It was frigid that night, and it snowed on the cat.

ADOLESCENT SELF-PITY IS WHERE IT ISN'T

Tonight, there's no foundation.
I'm a bag of skeletal confusion—
pouting fabrics of mud and pose,
poisonous music, dying crows.

Today was wrong, no pure answer,
head peeled down, I dreaded cancer.
Maybe the beat was snare drum bone
written in clouds, a wearisome tune.

Acquired nonsense, this bilious review.
I'm a curse: half-Catholic, half-Hebrew.
No poem or songs. No hope. Black tears.
I'm sorrow's blood, infected years.

Time to enjoy that sleep-sour death:
to die, to bleed, to lose God's breath?
I'll cushion the breast of a wounded bird,
its fractured wing, its hope—absurd.

BABY WHEN I THINK OF YOU
I THINK SYSTOLIC

sugar and honey mixed with vinegar love, being cuffed
with garter belts on tight drunken nights blindfolded in
jail, police chases through weeds, heart-shaped dandelions,
lunges into hot fudge clouds and meringue pillows the size
of small boulders, Kubla Khan's vibrating colors mixed with
cranberries and oranges, visions of hymenoptera stings
soaked in perfumed tincture of lemon juice, Krispy Kreme
donuts, X-rated whiskey sours on rocks of ancestors'
covenants, tree play where we prayed to join stacks of stone
pleading lives we didn't know, running chords of mistruths
and stealing cave flames, leopards and tigers racing across
operating room floors, yellow-eyed brown thrashers
repeating tunes of flowering buds, lenticular green skies
of toxic love-pox, infected midgets in shamanic masks,
Moby Dick, Peter Pan, Gunga Din, a trap door
leading to the infinite series of dark stairs, fireflies
lighting up knee kisses, Flannery O'Connor drinking
Schnapps, rusted shotguns pointing muzzles at the moon,
Bogart's dog eyes, Ingrid's hair, guitar strings on muddy stages,
doomsayers at biker rallies, tattooed songs of Lorca,
sunrises over evenings' lake secrets, pollen-bee lasers cutting
snow angels, a humid hand whispering the plunder of Moses,
stripping naked inside mica and quartz, the pink-white
of a laurel blossom, Soupy Sales raining frogs onto dark
country roads, Gunsmoke re-runs, the heart's panegyric
thrumming my singed tired hands, your body's warm
gyroscopic vertigo, love-spun, falling softly, bifurcated.

POSTCARD

Life's not bad; fish sticks & tartar sauce from: mayonnaise, ketchup, pickle relish. She likes Boone's Farm wine, Deviled Ham, Kraft Macaroni Dinner, instant iced tea. Beads hang from doorway. Carole King sings; two chairs fit kitchen table, guests take hall. Used green carpet, 9 x 12. Marriage makes you think. Aqua Velva drifts from Apt. 13, oil of wintergreen from crippled ballerina below. Mattress on floor supports vigorous love. We've got a friend with James Taylor. City stays thick where rent is cheap. Pigeons cluck outside sills. We measure days with Star Trek re-runs, cherry pie. We cram for exams. Woman in henna wig leaves gas on; she's hair-net crazy, demon eyes. We do laundry, three floors down. Some nights no heat, but real good love. Loud El trains. Homesick? Not with the Doors. This is the best goddamn time. Induction physical next week. Where's Saigon on map?   Love, J

HISTORY

You weren't about wedding planners
or doughnut-sized engagement rings.
I liked you for that, and the well-seasoned
frozen crab cakes from Mrs. Paul's kitchen.
You didn't care for rock and roll although
you slept with a piece of George Harrison's
sock between your sheets, a gift from his mum.
You didn't require courtship other than
sweet coleslaw, hot pastrami, Hires Root Beer,
and boxes of Screaming Yellow Zonkers.
We walked the darkness of Castor Avenue
checking rugs and lamplight we'd never own.
If I wrote your sad corpuscles' suffering tears
I'd be blind as a muffin rising in a stove.
I've omitted dreams of adjectives, breath nouns.
I've left out portfolios of tax records and spicy
wandering villanelles. I've left out three words.

ANNIVERSARY

Bouffage howdy-wife
my half-marrow light
bed purfle slut grate
let's go out tonight
flowers in hand
chocolates melting down
your shaved stewed prones
as my elf-locks dretch
your devilshine my fairhead
dream-hole sopping wet
and light heart-spoon.

Let's be boyfriend girlfriend
the evening's middle muskin
me ripping your pulpatoons
swaying your kissing crust
to melodious Spanish poems
while the dazzled waiter
by his urging serves our quaggle
gravy fun trying not to blench
our batterfanged night of rush-ring
frenzy our lovet's intimate
touching and my expanding
glox plumpers flesh-spaded carked
beneath the linen tablecloth.

HERE'S TO SAY

I am blessed with light reflected from your lips.
But I like your hips as compass handlebars.
There's no courage for my love. If you attempt
to scratch my eyes out with fingernail nouns
I'll harbor no scourge. I reside in the gel of my head,
and your love brings sleep like a cricket's song does.
If you're sad, I'll willow your shadow beside a dry pond.
Your heart mirrors its rhythms, a pulse in my ear.
When you slide your finger beneath my hair
it beats Sappho's lyrics and rough angels' wings.
Your sadness brings water and taproots my chest.
You center my doubt as to why life must bend.
Your sweat is cloud-pure, your legs pine mist gold.
I am Shiva or Satan, doing stand-up routines.
Your rage pulls lightly. I'm your dog on a chain.
You're the voice of peach nectar, a deep red wine.
I'm morning's black coffee, the *New York Times*.
You're lit scented candles, my first crème brûlée.

RIFTS

THE LESSON

Imagine the basement elevator
where laughter ends.
Forget the trees and sky of summer.
Imagine students' gleaming eyes—
new stethoscopes, bleached jackets
the color of sails. In the corner:
a chainsaw, scrubbed clean. Imagine
the dead wrapped in plastic sheets,
enormous loaves laid out on tables.
Imagine what their hands have forgotten.
Peel the oily shroud. Banish childish shadows
from inside your head.
No fangs or pentagrams. No curved horns.
Just organs, teeth, disconnected maps
of veins and bundled nerves.
Imagine no smiles, the puzzle of loss,
a nameless blue member empty of steam.
Embrace the heft of bone, the formalin—
an eternal toxic cologne. Beneath
buzzing fluorescent lights
imagine baptism's sponge
washing away final dirt, the sun
folded into decades of worthless words
rinsed then dried from pallid skin. Leave.
Return. Spill your coffee over the abdomen.
The yellow body won't withdraw.
Something cleansed away the reflex spasm.
Imagine scalpels approaching the plexus
buried beneath the arm. Imagine
the skin's last resistance. Every piece
becomes your own, except for the eyes.
Imagine what they say: You belong.

ON-CALL INSTRUCTIONS,
STATE HOSPITAL, 1985

Blessed are the poor in spirit, for theirs
is the kingdom of illness. Here live the stiff and gray,
yet the wind chimes of God sing like doves.
You must whisper these halls unless you have training.
Let your eyes become litmus paper lanterns and words.
See around corners like a clairvoyant dog.
Prepare for the holy reflux bible. Lights may turn
pink or colorless, don't worry. Drink black coffee in waves.
Button your coat of white linen. Wear three sturdy shoes.
Discover blue lamps that swell your heart's rhythm.
Socks should absorb your tourniquet troubles.
Accept the corridor of trap-door faces. Infiltrate your pockets
with the body's subway system. Bring electromagnets.
Cajole hemostats. Avoid tarragon-flavored scissors.
Write a thesaurus for a Martian poet whose moon is purple.
Palpate childhood's nightmares again;
then catalogue rivers around the Circle of Willis.
Forget treason. Honor the plague of unending restraints.
Absorb dry spit of pseudo-Aramaic. Plan for earlobes
and caged window traces. Bow to voltage and satellite dishes.
Arm yourself with needles, syringes of the Gospels,
so you can memorize missing chapters
from the *Manual of Therapeutics*. When a chest
smokes its serum, treat the underlying clause.
Chalk your reflex hammer to the angle of madness.
Praise zinc oxide powder. Sing psalms of proper catheters.
Prescribe bismuth similes for stomachs of nurses.
Will you default, or join in the syndrome? Forget
the screams of a thousand fingers, buried inside these walls.
Weep behind a badly painted door.
Pray you'll never hear when lobsters speak in tongues.
Devour your key, it's lightly salted.

FRACTURE LINES

First the claws approach your flinching throat.
Something without name forecloses your smile.
The darkness clown leaves no mercy or joke,
no old jalopy horn or country-western song
with lyrics of how everybody goes down the ring.
It's just what? Dozens, thousands, millions—flat.
On a distant hill—poplar leaves turn gold. Arrowed
ibises fly parallel to a speeding Chevrolet.
The glass vase melts and the desert is wilting
into breath-colors of a wide starless dream.
Not even a trace of the Milky Way's pallor of hope.
Soon the claws become victors: they judge the case.
And the old mirror doesn't recognize what you see.

FOR THOSE WHO LIVED
IN THE BACK WARDS

I pray for Paul with mercury skin
obsolete in vegetable knuckles,

and for Bernadette who sliced her abdomen
as if it were a baked potato begging sour cream.

Lord, put them back together again.
Don't let French fries go to waste, or spoil a tuna.

As for the pirate boy and subterranean woman
urged on by extraterrestrial opera stars,

let them procreate new forms of radar antennae.
I ask You to stop all flagella rounds in bushes.

No need for twisted aching supplicants.
Hold their ears, Lord, their nights awake, restrained.

Let them sleep like narcoleptic cat-men and women.
Love them, Lord, seize their unheard hourly prayers.

LOBOTOMY WARD RIDERS

Think about the bird-men lulled in the jelly-zoo.
Mull plate-glass windows and steel door hinges
when all there is to do is fight with the nurses.
Sneak out of restraints. Seek love in the call room
but gyre beyond black and white TV stations.
Eviscerated nomads squeeze over earlobes.
Barn-hills drive into adjoining eye chambers.
Demons prepare the holy serpents' metronomes.
Everyone preaches to the stale air's cadence.
Attendants in uniforms snap shoulder side-buttons,
reminding sweaty palms and nicotine-fingers.
From gray skin tubules and sticky neuronal fire,
forgotten groins dampen the fixed wingless angels.
On a shelf inside the third floor's cabinet
fourteen sterile ice picks gleam in unison.
As the noon whistle blows, the autoclave waits
for that one steady hand to arrive at Building Six.

POST-OP

Out of the depths: heart, water, string.
Where's the meaning in a glassful of bone?

Wheeled feet first from a green-tiled wing.
Everything efficient. Stories unknown.

The surgery team sutured four twisted roots
to a damaged graft of a hitchhiking dog.

Coy flocks unmasked, yet birds sing truth.
Misbegotten nests of hairballs and rag.

What can begin with a conversational prayer
and end holding séance in a chalice of tea?

Thirst, rain, seeds—precise dolor.
A first washed crawl toward intimate me.

Death strums guitar in the polished walls.
Or is life chasing voltage with a scalpel blade?

And how God is sighing, playing it all.
Ignoring *en passant*? Planning checkmate?

LOCKED WARD LADY

Through steel screen doors

you ripped out chickens

from beneath your abdomen,

rocked in the cold corner

by the mustard tile wall.

The sharp-headed pencil boy

and the mute cowboy's coffee

were hard cigarette spirals

and tiny germ fornications

inside the dirty deal's hourglass.

When you sat on tired screams

of ivy-covered plaster and spine—

oh, the blood wine,

the sinister whiskey,

the baked fruit of vendettas

turning a dream mosque

inside your perished eyes.

How it all made sense to Christ,

to the Buddha,

to those well-armed guards.

SOMEDAY YOU'LL LOSE A PATIENT

Think yellow fields whispering: Van Gogh.
Faceless smiles haunt faceless dreams.

You can't predict who—crutches are invisible.
A total eclipse surrounds your courage.

Then—of stagger and gray: insulate the news.
Someone asks, Did he pay his bill?

Robins jump from dogwood branches, swivel.
Hours teach magnolia leaves to curl.

As if the Lord had never come to Charleston.
As if nothing reaches into every language.

BRINGING THEM BACK

No easy matter for Lord Christ & Lazarus to smile in a cave
or for Mr. D—who folded his Lucky Strike pack
into his T-shirt sleeve close to tan skin like a love note
scolded by his wife he worked the biceps factory hard
swallowed Seagram's shots for love burn & when I asked
Did you ever kill anybody during the war Mr. D—?
nine years old was I on the lower steps & hard cement
lips callow I didn't know it was Gunsmoke's time shift
adamantine were his blue eyes alive until that darkness
began signs & the El sang pole dirges pigeons clucked he said
D- d- d- d- don't you ever ask anyone that question again
in sadness & rage of observance I saw Mr. D— 's torso
begin cachectic strolling the avenue sidewalks he swelled into
back alleys near Kresge's Five & Dime dated mattress mites
& lice scraps of lunchroll later on between taut cyclone fences
with homeless pigeons Mr. D—'s *caput medusae* abdomen
was fabled soon in the Frankford Hospital emergency room
lids jagged tasteless canned soup creamed corn pork & beans
nightly didn't survive his pancreatic song & years of yellow
green bile hepatic omentum whiskey spine & bursa death lasted
into gift lessons of other vets speaking G-clef stuttering verses
now I hear ligament & bone thrusts in nightmare's blood speech
I see Mr. D—'s Spanish moss beard floating in vodka rooms
I find buffalo sockets scratching torn holes over desert wadi
& night-colors matching red despair of the hunted crab hands
but I'll never ask another veteran that stuck question that bezoar
I've learned to shift down red to cerulean until misery shines
from cold depths & I wait & want to look as if each cell might again
wake & one day crawl & dance & even weep & rise like a psalm.

BEYOND THE PERFUME RIVER

after Issa

Napped—against policy for jungle-rot lieutenants.

Half the men fell into darkness like dying stars.

The day: of ordinary bug dreams. I miss my wife.

No one cools inside searing leaf and brass sweat.

Punished by sky-flowers, my living and dead and

Me. Surrounded by wire. No kind words from God.

8 A.M. RALPH H. JOHNSON V.A. MEDICAL CENTER

You'd think they'd take on the look of leaves,
torn branches. Few arrive with shrapnel scars,
their tours inscribed on baseball caps instead.
So much noise in their eyes.
Each skull contains that common electrical cloud.
They slide their bodies along morning's press
like old skates drifting over steel-hard ice.
And the one they call Jack arrives every day.
He shakes from scalp to toenail without control,
a monument rattled by a distant bomb.
Elevator doors open
like those of spaceships landing on a lawn.

IN THE MIDDLE OF THE BENCH

After Carlos Drummond de Andrade

In the middle of the bench there was a black patch and cane

there was a black patch and cane in the middle of the bench

there was a black patch and cane

in the middle of the bench there was a black patch and cane.

Clenched in my unblinking eyes

I'll never forget that in the middle of the bench

there was a black patch and cane

in the middle of the bench a black patch and cane.

WALLS OF THE CLINIC

What kind of turtle comes in, poking his M-16 head,
a café-au-lait-splotched cheek? Bullet-wound skin,
aged for years in culverts and woods, he's damn glad
ain't been ordered to Iraq. What are hair maps, he asks,
and clavicles of love? He's outlived smoke-shadows,
liquor, drugs. His dun head settled, 12-stepped a year.
O'Doul's removed splinters from his heart's plastic cup.
Learn from his friend. Bunk in a room, hide from stars.
Inside a month they'll be camping streets again.
Red camellias play against his dark-colored leaves.
How symptoms oblige to be stone-held ears.
In coats and layers, he cracks seven neck bones,
rubs his beard-lice, then finger-claws the universe.
He's retired young dreams in fields of Khe Sanh.
The ringing withdraws to its hard, hearty shell.
Spring birds flitter in oak trees and lay.
Refer him downstairs, Ms. Quinn, third floor.
Lean your chair against the hard taupe wall.
Drown together in the stomach of the world.

CRYSTAL

Nodding,

the paroled lizard-face

passes in a Lexus LS 460 sedan.

Your thoughts, behind, run uphill.

The dark-eyed pignut rolls

trans-retinal

through silence of the downward asphalt

until the solitary shell ceases

three feet short of hickory's fate.

Where you slice errant weeds,

ankle-deep green,

frictionless,

a Golem's nictitating eye-roots

scan candles and wine.

Now the rapid blaze of forehead is on,

Aleph's thread re-alphabetized,

zip-lined,

mad-forms ignite the uncrumbling

fissured lips soundless over clay.

Untrammeled, the orgy-guise

breeds inside your pulse again.

TELEMENTAL RELUCTANCE

A mind sorts absence in an office space stew.
Memos pin cork-space in thoughts from sound.
Again, they activate the fire alarm.
Afternoon's announcement returns faithfully:
We've completed all repairs on God's meridian clock.
Away from the lens, look at a book.
Return to technology's deadeye stare.
Whiskers, dark, uncork the head.
Lean skin unfolds into keloid scar.
Eyes: mosquitoes, Euphrates' blood.
Shoulders quake naptime from IEDs.
Young friends—viridian—mist below.
The missing fling curses to a soundproof Christ.
Breath and wadi. No teeth. No tongue.

THE SHIELD

Down Upper King Street Charleston
the gray-haired husky vet ignores
a needle and syringe thrown
into weeds behind the cyclone fence
his arm extends hand grips
a black aluminum alloy cane
morning shines upon twin titanium legs
ensconced inside his running shoes
he leads the dark-haired child
straddling a toy fire engine
with grubby yellow plastic wheels
all these molecules together flow
in a sequence precise like soldiers
inching toward an unexploded bomb
he the point man who diverts any fire
away from this girl's quotidian ride.

A NEW BEGINNING

The faceless man wrote to friends on Facebook.
They said he looked good in his black robe and shoes.
He'd been a handsome soldier. It was hard to look.

I imagined him as a kid with a comic book
studying caped superheroes who'd never lose.
He'd joined Special Forces. Now alien, his look.

He wiped—that chin—with his elbow's crook.
He posted if he wanted to; his right to choose.
I couldn't quite find him. It took

my breath. He explained his ex: she baked and cooked.
Heather loved his passion, their mutual tattoos.
She adored his bullmastiff. His spirit? Hooked.

Then orders to Kabul. Heather changed her looks.
She morphed into a cougar no man could refuse.
He came back a hero. She forsook

his heart. When he aimed at himself, his fingers shook.
He typed on the keyboard: should've used a noose.
The faceless man wrote to friends on Facebook.
He'd been a handsome soldier. I had to look.

NO TIME FOR AMERICAN IDOL

The prosthesis barks orders to the son:
Stay in the house! Watch out for bombs!
Leishmaniasis lives in the sandbox!

The boy goes looking for silver planes,
a blue-soda sky, flight patterns of spiders
and yellow jackets. T-shirts are chainmail suits,
sneakers heavy boots of silver armor.
The child fast-pedals his bike,
jousting Spanish moss that hangs
from thick oak shoulders and arms.

What cleanses the silence of a broadcast wound
assigned to a wife by the spit of war?
She asks few questions, wears avulsions every day,
stammers into morphine-papered walls.
She irons tears onto clothes,
strains syllables through colanders,
boils a husband's grief in chicken broth and time.

He'd welcome the Baghdad Boil on his calf again.
Sand flies pulse inside his missing leg.
At night it crawls along thick carpet
searching for a battlefield, and in the sights
laces up a polished leather ice skate.
Inside the rink of whiskey dreams and uniforms
it glides on bones of childhood.

The man knows the acid love of God.
His leg, disassembled in Mosul,
simply prays for giving up.

QUIZZES

How is your epistle uploaded? Are you the doctor?
Yes, I'm the doctor, a psychiatrist.
Do sand caves come from poetry stars?
Would you kindly tell me what month it is?
Apostolic verses derive from the ancients.
Do you know the name of this place?
The V.A. Hospital. St. Paul wasn't your patient.
Can you count back from 100 by 7s, please?
Why not ask me how the moon landed
on earth and became night's striptease?
Your record indicates three tours in Afghanistan.
Yes, Job. And I only have escaped alone to tell thee.
Do you have any appetite? Lost any weight?
Gilgamesh told me, Throw grits on a nurse.
How is your memory? Can you concentrate?
You aren't Gabriel and I don't believe the verse
where you whispered to Mary's holy veil.
Can you tell me the name of the president?
Job, you must read *The Angel's Manual of Style*.
Do you use cocaine? Huff any paint?
Some believe Barabbas means shame.
Why did you break that fluorescent bulb?
I damaged the ceiling flapping wing-pain.
Have you felt good enough to work in a job?
The moon is hungover from drinking earth's tears.
Do you hear voices inside your head?
Stained-glass windows, blood-shaped wars.
I want you to remember three things: Car. Apple. Bed.
My hands will heal logs burning in a stove.
Forget those three things. How's your mood?
Like I waltzed Bukovina from Cyclops love.
In your mind, are you sad, up, down, scared?
In the name of the Father, Son, and Holy Lip.

Are you having any weakness or discomfort?
Jacob, I'm strong enough to dislocate your hip.
How about homicidal or suicidal thought?
Dopamine opens a frequency to the Lord.
Can you tell me what month we're in?
Do you know what sins our fathers forged?
Have you heard of a medicine called lithium?
Salt of the earth. I take pepper with it.
Can you take some lithium for me?
Ask Lot's wife. She cooks with sea salt.
Any questions for the clinical team?
Can aerodynamic wings praise scapular dust?
I'm not sure. We're here to help you cope.
I'm deaf, dumb, blind. Enlightened like Oedipus.
Can you see that helicopter flying over the rooftop?
A holy dragonfly, Ezekiel's rotor blades.
Do you have any concerns?
When do I get out of seclusion? I'm saved.
Talk to Sarah the nurse, and Dr. Holtz, your intern.
Where do I wash my pile of soiled feathers?
Sarah will explain how things work on the unit.
I'm dragging full sorrow, God's golden zither.
See you tomorrow. We'll help you tune it.

ANTI-GRAVITY

By the federal porcelain stall, I hear a voice

coming from the meditation chapel next door.

"Hello, hello," the soft words repeat seven times.

Is a stranger over there, speaking out to God

or is God addressing me through the wall?

From a photograph on a desk, one little boy smiles.

Yet the computer only hums indifference.

Online, the *New England Journal of Medicine*

is either for or against high-deductible wisdom.

And the government, blindfolded like a hostage,

goes blank inside its marble colonnade.

The veteran scratches his ears, donates a dream.

But who answers the mountain's grieving lullaby?

If the middle class is merely thing, why clock in at all?

Everyone hears the beat of time's dull ring.

We misalign—like planets, with no mutual pull.

STAND DOWN

October. Lackawanna Boulevard. 82 degrees.
Driving, I see a homeless tall Marine
wearing camo pants, a gray T-shirt, tan boots.
Gesticulating, he talks to sparrows and tree roots.
I know him from the Veterans' Hospital.
I want to offer a ride, but . . .
He may be St. Francis, or he might slice off my head.
Nothing but kindness should be this hard.

HOMELESS VETERANS
UNDER THE OVERPASS

Watch ruby-throats lick nectar from stones.
Money spiders spin spasmodic graphs.
Stage-owls scream the road's expectation.
Lantana breathes sandstorms into empty mouths.

Guesses derive from Earth's morning hunger.
Nouns linger with indigo sounds.
Dawn hoists the moon-face glowing backward.
An osprey relaxes above the water.

They recover their best on cardboard marquees.
Eye-tetrahedrons slip tongues without mercy.
The wind believes their gray-shaped voices.
This thunder is given its name.

WHEN TECHNOLOGY GOES DOWN

Don't work the end of a dusty hall. Your room is like an empty confessional, begging its priest to return.

Moles shoot paintball from their maze in the yard. Below the marl, a psychologist eats hard candy. Something therapeutic nails indifference. "All right, goodbye," he says, and disconnects.

The chasuble chases the alb. Someone yells, Patroclus, watch out! If every war isn't swallowed hard, Achilles will shoot his mother's best friend.

A woman acts like a blind person who is trying to gather every atom of a broken mercury thermometer. A dead man writes his living will.

With your elbow braced on a desk, crooked and light, weep like a man who's had a stroke. Spreadsheets help faithless accept their fate—the same as Schrödinger's cat. Try to grow vineyards in a box, or perhaps some lettuce or chard.

A scientist studies the hippocampus. He finds a new dendritic nook. He can't comprehend the form of a tree. Why must the fax be asleep? Wait for God's answer, His bureaucratic grappling hook.

APOCALYPTIC DRONE

Of course you don't want to die,
but the drone is coming today.
The drone that delivered your meals, Amen.
The one that pressure-washed your house,
walked your three poodles,
and trimmed your azaleas and sago palms.
The drone is coming today.
It delivered three call girls
and Viagra to your home last week.
By now you've received
those benzodiazepines to ease your fear of laserization.
It's already towed away your driverless car.
Your lupus? Too costly to treat.
As you require dental implants to chew a good steak,
your work is done, your strength is weak.
Remember, you voted for this in 2019.
The drone is coming today.
Repeat the phrase, *thy rod and thy staff* . . .
These words shall bring solace your way.
The drone is soon to arrive, Amen.
Smile. Laugh. Profess your last prayer.
Relax. Rest. *Dulce et decorum est.*
The drone is coming today.

SYNTHESIS

NEAR THE SUMMIT: AUTUMN

Ironweed—dried.
Butterflies half-fed
And this blood-red turn
of Whiteside Mountain's
maple leaf tree
makes me see
for the first time
how an afternoon dies.

TO CROCUS, FROM CALAMUS

If you Wiki my sun
I'll Wiki your shade.

Astilbe. Coreopsis. Hosta.
How your carbon fingers reach my dirt.

The warm sky yells drunken invitations.
Water forms and soaks our bone-skins dry.

I am apt to fall toward your ankles.
I report to Shiva lies of wicked truth.

If you build a fence around your text
I'll forever dance a groping Amaryllis.

Your silent drops are sea-smell rain.
The dogwood sings, Where's the phlox?

If I Wiki your thigh
Will you Wiki my tongue?

You turn me cruciform—
like Vitruvian Man in detox.

OCTOBER STILL

Three purple dry hydrangea flowers stand

projecting claims against the coming front.

Yet morning haze can't stabilize demands

derived from yellow falls. How fast a blunt

wind reappears to work its swirling brush—

forms tessellated matter, colored weaves.

Abscission cells must subjugate. They crush

against the chlorophyll. Fog-figures cleave.

Sienna pleated remnants, stalks and stems

begin to wrinkle down like unstitched clothes.

Few katydids, disorganized, grate—send

last signals. Boulders slow-dissolve below

impatient clouds. Entropic me. Breath drone.

Arranged, I sip sweet coffee. Pencil down.

THIN LINE SEQUENCE

Grief drives in waves. Our son dreams victims' parts.
One gray cold pasty lip. A stellate wound.
Occipital-pierced bones, heat-peeled. Stunned hearts.
Bad dreams on diapered kids half-dressed, scold-bruised
sad hues, dark like plums. Old gash, hard shoe kicks—
matched ecchymoses—coroner-described.
Once face, now shorn, below I-26—
how does he place the swell's unbroken tide?
Cop business: lies. Lascivious facts. Vid-
eo clips. Mind-cannibals. Addict zones.
Clipped missing arm. Eyes swollen. Juice-foam. SIDS.
Wit-hidden, hell-stripped. Stiff Kevlar vest home.
Cuffs. Asp. How semi-automatics dull.
Flash. Recoil. Shuttled tears. 911 call.

BATTLE CRY
OF THE SECULAR JEWISH MOTHER

Not afraid to use bay leaves and salt
she knows ancient techniques
cannot be resisted.
Fresh mushrooms, basil,
roast beef with garlic gravy
and noodles dusted
in freshly grated Romano cheese
will make you abandon
your wish for self-protection.
Hot buttery cornbread
tastes of the child's discrete winter.
Roasted chicken basted with paprika broth
charms your stomach into yielding secrets.
A few glasses of Pinot, iced club soda and whiskey,
and her warrior pace bubbles,
widens as you fall beneath the weight
of leg of lamb, mint jelly, stuffing with raisins.
You can identify with *sarmale*,
how a coat of cabbage swells from steaming
beef and rice, how it heats from inside
instinctively. She knows the quickening
your heart-flesh makes
when it is lonely for meatballs
bathed in sweet tomato sauce and onions.
Then the mercy march of your struggle fails
to iceberg lettuce, red peppers,
bleu cheese dressing and croutons.
Your strength to resist wanes
as you shamelessly trade in your waist
for another warm crêpe
filled with brandied cherries and heavy cream.
After two cups of coffee and three liqueurs,
a tray of French cheeses,

she lays out freshly baked kugel
and bowls of chocolate ice cream.
Before sleep, you remember who you were
when she first captured you and made you sit,
made you plead for the slow end to arrive,
for that disappointment in her eyes to go away.

SIX TIMES ZERO

At 83, Father explains that his childhood shoes
were hand-me-downs passed through the family's
4 out of 10 siblings—Augie, John, Eddie, and Joe—
before staking his rightful footwear claim.
As a boy he'd patch 2 outsoles with cardboard inside.
I visualize 5 + 5 toes, little father feet, how long wires
of a surgeon scraped that 9-year-old's shin-bone infection.
When I was small, his equation was misunderstood.
I couldn't walk beside him 1-to-1 on paved streets
of Frankford Avenue, so I'd hover behind his pace
like a helium-filled balloon knotted to
the back of a red hook-and-ladder truck roaring
toward a multi-alarm blaze from the Foulkrod station.
And Father's irritable fear was that I'd scuff
the uppers of his spit-shined size 7 shoes. Every
evening he'd spread the *Daily News* open across
the cellar floor to catch brown flakes of KIWI wax
scattered fine by the Empire horsehair shoe brush.
Some nights by my bed: sober, funny, not insane,
he'd recite multiplication tables then mumble
a lament: Should've stayed in school past 6th grade.
Then I, his sonny metronome, corrected mistakes.
Half-block away, the El rumbled along the line.
But tonight, he cannot recall the product of 6 x 0.
What does a change in the math signal imply?
Maybe something fallen from a sturdy branch,
a blue jay, stiff and gone from the Nile virus?
But I wouldn't even bet a poem on it. Perhaps
he is rubbing 2 sticks into my clinical mind.
Before he hangs up, he mentions some results:
a stress thallium test, repeated echocardiograms.
Something like the art of betting on numbers.
Something like a dance between breath-stones.
Something about fractions, a leak in his heart.

ALL THAT COMMOTION

Before bed, he lines up spice jars alphabetically.
Then he brushes his teeth.
For 6 years, he risked life daily to feed an alley cat.
He thinks this before he falls asleep.

Then he brushes his teeth.
He never misses a trick, they say.
Does he think this before falling asleep?
In the army, he had a 22 inch waist.

He never misses a trick, they say,
and at 84, he'll take 3 guys with his fists.
The Army built his biceps. He kept that 22 inch waist.
He checks the weather forecast 17 times a day.

Can an 84-year-old man beat 3 dudes with his fists?
As a kid, he stole anthracite to heat the family home.
He checks the weather 17 times a day.
He calls all politicians "Bums."

As a child, he stole coal from the mines for heat,
yet he starred in my childhood's nightmares.
He still calls politicians "Bums."
What's his favorite book? *The Farmer's Almanac.*

Disguised, he starred in my childhood's nightmares.
But he cried when he saw me near death.
His favorite book is *The Farmer's Almanac,*
Ortlieb's—his favorite beer.

He cried when he saw me half-dead.
For six years, he risked his life to feed an alley cat.
Ortlieb's was his favorite beer.
Before sleep, he lines up spice jars alphabetically.

EXILE

Last week, mother turned 94 and her soft-boned back
bent like a palmetto in a tropical storm, she fast-cooked
eggplant salad, 37 meatballs, a matzo kugel, *sarmale*,
cheesecake. When I was 8, she yelled, Leave home
and never return! Knick-knacked, paddy-whacked,
I screamed back: Leave it to Beaver! We weren't that
Frankenstein for reruns of *The Lone Ranger* minus
Silver and Tonto. I set out for the alley behind row houses,
stomped on every pavement crack, broke Mother's back.
White clover flowers fed fat bees, black and yellow,
milkweed trees shadowed clothes props, wives. Open
window TVs cheered the Phillies, the El train screeched
silver wheels above avenue windows. Street maggots
debrided a wino's leg. Lorenzo the stylist booked bets
on 2 pay phones, Italian opera blared as he winked girls.
Bus fumes stank, dogs chased cats chased dull pigeons.
I bought a pack of Pall Malls at Entwistle's Apothecary,
doubled-back to the concrete hole beside the Baptist church.
That space, 8 feet deep, covered by a hinged iron grating,
nearly fractured my fingers as I lifted, found toe-ledges,
jumped in, lowered bars as I fell. Like a holy jail inside—
airy so the dogs couldn't eat me. I feared winged monkeys.
Popeye was absorbed in a sea dream of anorexic women.
One drunk, suffering from polio, later pissed on my head.
I napped Oscar Meyer hot dogs, mugs of Hires Root Beer.
The eyeless sandman, my only friend that day, suggested
I borrow a push mower, clippers, 3-in-1 oil, canvas gloves;
I could trim 10 x 10 backyards. I puffed smokes. By 6 P.M.,
paddy-whacked, I climbed tobacco fog, gave a dog a bone,
this young man went rolling home. So Mom: 9/10 century,
I've stopped trudging alleys, sulking near hallowed holes.
I am Boris Karloff, Michael Rennie, Gort, gloved hands
of Eleanor Roosevelt, a SEPTA train rattling over I-95.
Call me a knight of green quiet rain. *Klaatu barada nikto.*

CONDOMINIUM DWELLERS, 2628 WELSH ROAD

They say they've lost their purpose, lost their depth.
The old are ways of doing things to stay alive.
Moving magazines from table edge to floor. Quoting
Reader's Digest. Dusting coils behind the fridge.

Screaming out philosophy of Guy Lombardo's
sugar dogs and singing killer cats. Saving broken glass.
Quoting motor oil's effects on DNA.
Testing pain's viscosity at minus 32 degrees.

Showing how to gap the plugs inside your head.
Slowing every other shouted word.
Shining Cole Haan shoes with mold, banana peels.
How to polish bathroom chrome with Barbasol.

Ways to fix a toilet leak with lemon juice and vinegar.
Watching for a fading nod, the inattentive blistered eye.
And when it's time for them to shop for breath, tomorrow
they will rise again, and sing like rain.

DERIVATIVES

Cells—little eyes spreading over sterile glass,
stretching tentacular arms that will touch,
jellyfish-like, elastic, clear,
and there, in the nucleus of one cell,
I see you, Zalman Segal, dear Uncle,
floating in your Jerusalem carpentry shop,
free of blue numbers tattooed in your arms,
having forgotten Transnistria's camps
but never forgiving anything else,
because everything real was a dream—
images from laughter's baritone voice,
a bird whistling from that Romanian tree
where you are standing, gray hat,
simple vest. I open life's flask of tears
and you watch as I gather them by pipette,
heat them in a pot for herbal tea
that you and I share with sweet things.

That you and I share with sweet things,
heat them in a pot for herbal tea
and you watch as I gather them by pipette—
simple vest, I open life's flask of tears
where you are standing, gray hat,
a bird whistling from that Romanian tree,
images from laughter's baritone voice,
because everything real was a dream—
but never forgiving anything else,
having forgotten Transnistria's camps,
free of blue numbers tattooed in your arms.
Floating in your Jerusalem carpentry shop,
I see you, Zalman Segal, dear uncle,
and there, in the nucleus of one cell,

jellyfish-like, elastic, clear,
stretching tentacular arms that will touch—
cells: little eyes spreading over sterile glass.

KING DAVID CEMETERY

Heading toward the creek, we bow to pines.
They form a black spiked fence.
Umbrellas of hickory trees
shadow cold bones, respectful
of weather's absence.

Mom, Dad, and I retain a crow.
We visit Malvina, Pese, Zalman, Marcel.
This is a different kind of motel
where sleep pays everything in advance.
We listen to the sky's verbs and nouns.

Dark beards and caps on yellow backhoes.
When innkeepers groan, prepare another room.
We plot speedy journeys, grass to sun.
Dad is ready for the casino. Mom readies her bones.
First we place bets: flat stones.

LIKE THE SILENCE BETWEEN STARS

When the brown rabbit skims
over granite stones across the sloped yard
and Cullowhee Mountain birds
mute their music as morning rises into 9 A.M.
you wonder how that black bear
appears from behind the rhododendron
without a single noise or grass blade bent
and like a poem without words
ambles past your bedroom window
below Buddha's glance and the purple leaf plum
leaving no scent or scat or tracks
then disappears through common daisies
downhill toward Gem Mine Creek
hidden by untrimmed laurels
the thrust of locust trees soon-to-fall.

BUBBE'S PILLOW

I can measure now
along the hypotenuse of sorrow

and what remains
is 15 by 15 inches square.

Strange to have ignored this treasure,
6 years blended to a rocking chair.

At last, I've brought you home,
placed beside the wooden frame,

crimson blankets as friends.
How occupied, the inside air.

Background cloth, a pea soup field.
Chicory and lily pearls.

A quatrain of flowers, fingers,
knotted glasses on that European face.

The fingertips' embroidery
prays down from heaven's catch.

I watch you patch and sew again.
That silver-mended smile: Romanian.

BOUNDARY

I've been married so long
I can't tell which pain is my actual pain.
My wife cannot sleep or cry,
her blood-tears are strained alone
and grief does not fry or sauté easily.
She reads the electrical sponge
in brain salt that sprinkles and carries
all night, all life, until the incense
of our voltage shorts-out,
then death do us part, Amen.
That's why I carry parts of her shadow—
one leg, one arm, and the root
of her torso's suffering.
But I can't relieve the sorrow
abandoning her umbilicus
or the heart-span about to burst
like a water balloon behind her chest wall.
Her mother has died
after 90 years full of emptiness.
There's no need to carry that, my wife says.
It's too large a silence
held in check by time's serrated knife,
its toothed conversation.

HOW VOICE LEECHES TIME

I'm trying God-speak between headstones.
I'm trying slant rhymes inside bony stables.
Roy St. John, orderly-mentor, taught me to wrap the dead.
I'm trying to hear this information
from behind hospital curtains
invading my dreams.
I pack something firm, found.

I'm edging toward a coyote's demise.
I'm edging toward gray-stiff neck fur.
Alabaster fangs glower against my deck.
I'm edging distal to a fly-winged absence,
placing canine teeth inside plastic shrouds.
I stuff the unknown frozen dirt.
How wind blows sand over beaches.

I'm thinking moon-teeth shattering poems.
I'm thinking physics of water burned into melt
at Fukushima Daiichi.
I'm thinking sacred deer of Nara,
how they bow before smiling temple children.
Who tests English word pronunciations?
Giant Zen bells suffering over Kyoto.

I'm considering darkness reformed.
I'm considering 613 shadows, ancient songs
of uncut fields, ironweed and butterfly-bitten air.
I'm considering God's artistic explosions,
streaming weeds, how the bee-drift
howls the Psalms' missing words.
How breath from winter is cinnamon and dust.

LIGHTING CANDLES

Glowing amber shimmers, drawing four black bars against
the vinyl wall behind a plastic chair. Night—the prison of living.
Mother dream-walks unfamiliar mountain terrain.
Thousands of men—naked—piled upon roadsides.
Waxy legs, splayed like felled trees. She tries to scream
but can't make sound. Whose dream is this, mother asks.
She worries over Father, who stays late in the kitchen,
recording when the refrigerator compressor goes off and on.
He never writes, she complains, not even three words
to his only son. A pen generates text, loses ink.
We no longer estivate. Bones are vexed.
Pese, Ianchu, Zalman, and Rubin lift fingers
to light another candle tucked inside a broken glass.
A great horned owl breaks the silence.

IT IS WHAT IT IS

Those fingertips of Keats you want to understand.
To beseech the oak the way you touch your lover's hair.
To comprehend a mockingbird's insomnia.
Night birds pipe tunes instead of eating Ambien.
Memorize villanelles straight from their beaks.
Do fallen willows create the manubrium of a breastbone?
Avian trills outside the window encourage you to speak from sleep.
Change to a word orbiting earth above white clouds.
The oceans banish bones into corners and krill.
Yet centipede grass plows roots across the sandy soil.
Why complain in the midst of apples?
And where the hell are all the dead?
Understand the video of Dr. John Keats, his fear that he'll cease.
Even disembodied fingers grapple with the hour of death.
Scientists believe 1.5 kilograms of bacteria colonize the human gut.
But which shape leads a dance with 3.3 pounds of flora?
Include the sum tango of germs sitting on the surface
or inside a person's frame; only 10% of all the cells
inhabiting a woman or man are human cells.
Where are the fingers that pray love's poems?
When we depart, where do heavy germs emigrate? Do they
exit like disgruntled parishioners leaving a church in ruin?
Can this imply the need for proper psalms?
Why did Achilles wash his grief with excrement?
When a faceless man borrows your face to hunt
the passing afternoon, wonder why you're 61.8% water by weight.
Perhaps the notion of a saint is more wet than dry.
Somewhere a red tin roof peels an old barn.
Mockingbirds are lonely odes
yet the eyelash of God is found in every horizon.
We are surely more than sex of stones.
Life becomes habitual sin and falling rain.
The motions of a pear sitting in a bowl.
Or maybe just a *hora* danced with angels keeping time.

REJOICE

Standing in the men's room next to the tall veteran
wearing a gray ball cap and balancing himself
beside his aluminum gray-handled federal cane
adjacent to the self-flushing porcelain receptacle
I think how funny it seems that we begin each day
pouring liquids into half-asleep corporeal selves
then meet and stand or sit next to lined strangers
as daylight and fluids return to somewhere else
and it's all right if we talk fundamental piss
precisely as the great Phillip Larkin once did
perhaps he realized we're mostly lunacy and sodium
fundamental universe stuff as I recall something
about cleaning up my father's urine puddle
that splashed over my sneakers and the waxed floor
of the hospital room on the day he came from the ICU
he had barely stood with my mother holding
a plastic bottle before his groin and I steadying him
with both hands pinning that ridiculously tailored
hospital gown so that the micturition act could be made
his warm spray returned like some carnival baptism
yet we laughed as no one else had time or thought
to pull the polymeric lid off the goddamn bottle
so that his life-stream ricocheted across the floor
beneath the bed and soaked my father's rented socks
my mother's long black coat my Reebok shoes
such relief we possessed magnificent to witness
how a gray-headed eagle was nursed back to flight
after damage to wings over the dark sea's reflection
we found moon-tears and love's bitter salt.

GRIEFDRIFT

Singe the holy burn cloud.
Grasp its absent day-weight and why-chain.
Deep charts arouse His immanence here.
Where challah meets wafer, find three.
And the terrible whimpering of God

flamedarks a wild yeast there.
Lossthreads fail the buttonholes.
Before dampest Christ
above darkness corridors
below cushioned knee-glare

carpals churn the raging eye.
Tumbling root, nebulized stone,
tear-squalls nick the heart-back.
Cicatrix the angels half-spilled.
Bring clock-rooms, if-breath. Dust-play.

ANNIVERSARY OF A QUESTION

Fully effaced, spring delivers its infant head,

pink beyond the dewy geometric bridge,

while two gulls couple the light.

Together forty-three years,

those loving kids had thrived

on things both small and large,

heaters warmed by steam compressed.

Third floors cooled their innocence.

Some argued bitter nights. Mad are dreams

of sweetness nicked, returned yet grasped,

then swallowed, bashed, deep-stirred

to quicksand's nature, pluperfect's past.

JUST PASSING THROUGH

Ordinary, one's death, yet different from anything
you've ever lived through.
　　　　　—Costika Melchiu

There's a breach in the works.
The pendulum stopped, congealed.

I remove its arms, strip numbers away.
Single digits: placed on a silver table.
Double digits: dumped in a plastic can.

I weigh the empty face,
clean its expression with a vinegar sponge
stolen from a Rilke poem.

Tyler, my grandson,
asks if I believe in reincarnation.
I'll return as an osprey, he says.

And I'll be a porpoise in the ocean, I decide,
chasing fish to the surface for your mid-day meal.

Time to discuss sunset dreams, Cabernet sky.
Never drink and fly, I warn
and always protect your necessary beak.

Smiling, he goes to the yard, climbs an oak.
I remove number twelve from the plastic can.
The clock unwinds itself.

WHAT I AM TAKING HOME

The teal color, the black collar of my father's jacket.
The air around the aluminum cane he leans on
now that he can wield it like an M-1 with fixed bayonet.
Mother waving from the condo's second floor window
as if my son and I were embarking on a spaceship journey.
No buttered warm cornbread or a cherry cheesecake slice,
no purple borscht heavy with sour cream.
Maybe something from the cosmos, the blessings of their eyes.
An old Yiddish tune she sang before the Holocaust.
Dad as a child, hiding in Dirty Eddy's Bar—
watching Tuffy Craig pull a miniature Chihuahua
from the pocket of his old miner's coat.
How "Dog" wobbled the bar, licking a whiskey trail.
And the story of my grandfather, Joseph,
who wanted my father to learn the construction trade.
Too young, Dad looked up at the wooden scaffolding and cried,
I don't want to climb up there, Pop, I'm afraid!
Joseph pranced on the tallest angle of the roof,
laughing, kicking his feet, outlined in clouds.
Yes, my parents—like that. Dance steps on a beam.

ABOUT THE AUTHOR

Joseph Zealberg, M.D., received his undergraduate degree from Temple University and his medical degree from The Medical College of Pennsylvania, with residency training at the University of Virginia Medical Center in Charlottesville. As a psychiatrist, he works half-time in private practice in Charleston, South Carolina, and half-time at the Ralph H. Johnson V.A. Medical Center. He is also a clinical professor of psychiatry at the Medical University of South Carolina.

ABOUT THE ARTIST

Angela Zealberg graduated from the College of Liberal Arts of Temple University in Philadelphia in 1978, after which she pursued a long-standing interest in visual arts, studying drawing, painting, and printmaking. She lives near Charleston and is married to the author. They have one son and two grandchildren, both of whom attend universities in South Carolina.

ABOUT THE WORD WORKS

The Word Works, a nonprofit literary organization, publishes contemporary poetry and presents public programs. The Hilary Tham Capital Collection presents work by poets who volunteer for literary nonprofit organizations. Nomination forms are requested from qualifying nonprofits by April 15 and manuscript submissions from nominated poets by May 1. Other imprints include the Washington Prize, International Editions, and The Tenth Gate Prize. A reading period is also held in May.

Monthly, The Word Works offers free literary programs in the Chevy Chase, MD, Café Muse series, and each summer, it holds free poetry programs in Washington, D.C.'s Rock Creek Park. Annually in June, two high school students debut in the Joaquin Miller Poetry Series as winners of the Jacklyn Potter Young Poets Competition. Since 1974, Word Works programs have included: "In the Shadow of the Capitol," a symposium and archival project on the African American intellectual community in segregated Washington, D.C.; the Gunston Arts Center Poetry Series; the Poet Editor panel discussions at The Writer's Center; and Master Class workshops.

As a 501(c)3 organization, The Word Works has received awards from the National Endowment for the Arts, the National Endowment for the Humanities, the D.C. Commission on the Arts & Humanities, the Witter Bynner Foundation, Poets & Writers, The Writer's Center, Bell Atlantic, the David G. Taft Foundation, and others, including many generous private patrons.

The Word Works has established an archive of artistic and administrative materials in the Washington Writing Archive housed in the George Washington University Gelman Library. It is a member of the Council of Literary Magazines and Presses and its books are distributed by Small Press Distribution.

More information at WordWorksBooks.org.

FROM THE HILARY THAM CAPITAL COLLECTION

Mel Belin, *Flesh That Was Chrysalis*
Doris Brody, *Judging the Distance*
Sarah Browning, *Whiskey in the Garden of Eden*
Grace Cavalieri, *Pinecrest Rest Haven*
Christopher Conlon, *Gilbert and Garbo in Love*
      & *Mary Falls: Requiem for Mrs. Surratt*
Donna Denizé, *Broken like Job*
W. Perry Epes, *Nothing Happened*
Bernadette Geyer, *The Scabbard of Her Throat*
Barbara G. S. Hagerty, *Twinzilla*
James Hopkins, *Eight Pale Women*
Brandon Johnson, *Love's Skin*
Marilyn McCabe, *Perpetual Motion*
Judith McCombs, *The Habit of Fire*
James McEwen, *Snake Country*
Miles David Moore, *The Bears of Paris*
      & *Rollercoaster*
Kathi Morrison-Taylor, *By the Nest*
Michael Shaffner, *The Good Opinion of Squirrels*
Maria Terrone, *The Bodies We Were Loaned*
Hilary Tham, *Bad Names for Women*
      & *Counting*
Barbara Louise Ungar, *Charlotte Brontë, You Ruined My Life*
      & *Immortal Medusa*
Jonathan Vaile, *Blue Cowboy*
Tera Vale Ragan, *Reading the Ground*
Rosemary Winslow, *Green Bodies*
Michele Wolf, *Immersion*

OTHER WORD WORKS BOOKS

THE WASHINGTON PRIZE

Nathalie F. Anderson, *Following Fred Astaire*, 1998
Michael Atkinson, *One Hundred Children Waiting for a Train*, 2001
Molly Bashaw, *The Whole Field Still Moving Inside It*, 2013
Carrie Bennett, *biography of water*, 2004
Peter Blair, *Last Heat*, 1999
John Bradley, *Love-in-Idleness: The Poetry of Roberto Zingarello*,
       1995, 2ND edition, 2014
Richard Carr, *Ace*, 2008
Jamison Crabtree, *Rel[AM]ent*, 2014
B. K. Fischer, *St. Rage's Vault*, 2012
Ann Rae Jonas, *A Diamond Is Hard But Not Tough*, 1997
Frannie Lindsay, *Mayweed*, 2009
Richard Lyons, *Fleur Carnivore*, 2005
Fred Marchant, *Tipping Point*, 1993, 2ND edition 2013
Ron Mohring, *Survivable World*, 2003
Brad Richard, *Motion Studies*, 2010
Jay Rogoff, *The Cutoff*, 1994
Prartho Sereno, *Call from Paris*, 2007, 2ND edition 2013
Enid Shomer, *Stalking the Florida Panther*, 1987
John Surowiecki, *The Hat City After Men Stopped Wearing Hats*, 2006
Miles Waggener, *Phoenix Suites*, 2002
Mike White, *How to Make a Bird with Two Hands*, 2011
Nancy White, *Sun, Moon, Salt*, 1992, 2ND edition 2010

THE TENTH GATE PRIZE

Lisa Sewell, *Impossible Object*, 2015

INTERNATIONAL EDITIONS

Keyne Cheshire (trans.), *Murder at Jagged Rock: A Tragedy
    by Sophocles*
Yoko Danno & James C. Hopkins, *The Blue Door*
Moshe Dor, Barbara Goldberg, Giora Leshem, eds., *The Stones
    Remember: Native Israeli Poets*
Moshe Dor (Barbara Goldberg, trans.), *Scorched by the Sun*
Lee Sang (Myong-Hee Kim, trans.), *Crow's Eye View: The Infamy
    of Lee Sang, Korean Poet*
Vladimir Levchev (Henry Taylor, trans.), *Black Book of the
    Endangered Species*

ADDITIONAL TITLES

Karren L. Alenier, *Wandering on the Outside*
Karren L. Alenier, Hilary Tham, Miles David Moore, eds.,
    Winners: A Retrospective of the Washington Prize
Christopher Bursk, ed., *Cool Fire*
Barbara Goldberg, *Berta Broadfoot and Pepin the Short*
W.T. Pfefferle, *My Coolest Shirt*
Jacklyn Potter, Dwaine Rieves, Gary Stein, eds., *Cabin Fever:
    Poets at Joaquin Miller's Cabin*
Robert Sargent, *Aspects of a Southern Story
    & A Woman From Memphis*

CPSIA information can be obtained at www.ICGtesting.com
Printed in the USA
BVOW05s1725060415

394573BV00001B/2/P